Hippocrene
CHILDREN'S
ILLUSTRATED
PORTUGUESE
DICTIONARY

ENGLISH · PORTUGUESE
PORTUGUESE · ENGLISH

Compiled by the Editors of Hippocrene Books
Portuguese language translation and consultation by Joseph F. Privitera, Ph.D.

Interior illustrations by S. Grant (24, 81, 88); J. Gress (page 10, 21, 24, 37, 46, 54, 59, 65, 72, 75, 77);
K. Migliorelli (page 13, 14, 18, 19, 20, 21, 22, 25, 31, 32, 37, 39, 40, 46, 47, 66, 71, 75, 76, 82, 86, 87);
B. Swidzinska (page 9, 11, 12, 13, 14, 16, 23, 27, 28, 30, 32, 33, 35, 37, 38, 41, 42, 45, 46, 47, 48, 49, 50,
52, 53, 56, 57, 58, 59, 60, 61, 62, 63, 66, 68, 69, 70, 71, 72, 73, 75, 77, 78, 79, 83), N. Zhukov (page 8, 13,
14, 17, 18, 23, 27, 29, 33, 34, 39, 40, 41, 52, 64, 65, 71, 72, 73, 78, 84, 86, 88).
Cover photo © 2002 www.arttoday.com

Design, prepress, and production: Graafiset International, Inc.

Cataloging-in-Publication Data available from the Library of Congress.

ISBN 0-7818-0886-3

Printed in Hong Kong.

For information, address:
Hippocrene Books, Inc.
171 Madison Avenue
New York, NY 10016

INTRODUCTION

With their absorbent minds, infinite curiosities and excellent memories, children have enormous capacities to master many languages. All they need is exposure and encouragement.

The easiest way to learn a foreign language is to simulate the same natural method by which a child learns English. The natural technique is built on the concept that language is representational of concrete objects and ideas. The use of pictures and words are the natural way for children to begin to acquire a new language.

The concept of this Illustrated Dictionary is to allow children to build vocabulary and initial competency naturally. Looking at the pictorial content of the Dictionary and saying and matching the words in connection to the drawings gives children the opportunity to discover the foreign language and thus, a new way to communicate.

The drawings in the Dictionary are designed to capture children's imaginations and make the learning process interesting and entertaining, as children return to a word and picture repeatedly until they begin to recognize it.

The beautiful images and clear presentation make this dictionary a wonderful tool for unlocking your child's multilingual potential.

Deborah Dumont, M.A., M.Ed.,
Child Psychologist and Educational Consultant

Portuguese Pronunciation
A Reference Guide to the Dictionary

Letter	Pronounced
a	**ah** as in English 'c<u>a</u>r'
	ä, Ä as in 'c<u>a</u>t'
b	**b** as in English '<u>b</u>ar'
c	**k** before *a*, *o*, and *u*, as in English 'c<u>a</u>t'
	s before *e* or *i* as in English '<u>c</u>ircus'
ç	**s** before *a*, *o*, and *u*, as in English '<u>s</u>ay'
d	**d** as in English '<u>d</u>o'
e,ê	**eh** as in English 'm<u>e</u>t' when stressed: *com<u>é</u>dia* (koh-MEH-deeh-ah), *rêde* (REH dĭh)
	ĭh, short **ĭ** as in English 'h<u>i</u>t,' in a final vowel: *sab<u>e</u>* (SAH bĭh), *diss<u>e</u>* (DEEH- sĭh)
f	**f** as in English '<u>f</u>air'
g	**g** hard, before *a*, *o*, and *u*, as in English '<u>g</u>ame'
	zh soft, before *e* or *i*, as the *s* in English 'mea<u>s</u>ure,': *janela* (zhah-NEH-lah), *j<u>o</u>ta* (ZHAW-tah)
i	**eeh** as in English 'mach<u>i</u>ne'
j	**zh** as the *s* in English 'mea<u>s</u>ure,': *janela* (zhah-NEH-lah), jota (ZHAW-tah)
l	**l** as in English '<u>l</u>ake'
m	**m** as in English '<u>m</u>ay.' At the end of a word it indicates nasalization of the preceding vowel: *fal<u>am</u>* (FAHL-ahn)
n	**n** as in English '<u>n</u>o'
o	**aw** when stressed, as in English 'd<u>o</u>g,' 's<u>o</u>ft,': *n<u>o</u>ve* (NAW-veeh)
	ooh when unstressed, as in English 'b<u>oo</u>t,': *o filho* (ooh-FEEHL-yooh)
ou,ô	**oh** as in English 'l<u>a</u>w,' when stressed: *gang<u>o</u>rra* (gahn-GOH-řah), *tes<u>ou</u>ro* (teh-ZOH-rooh), *c<u>ô</u>rnos* (KOHR-noohs)
p	**p** as in English 'o<u>p</u>en': *p<u>é</u>* (PEH), *ma<u>p</u>a* (MAH-pah)
q	**k** as in English '<u>c</u>ar': *q<u>ué</u>* (KEH)
r,rr	**ř, Ř,** pronounced with a slight trill, with the tip of the tongue when written double, or before another consonant: *pa<u>r</u>te* (PAŘ-tĭh); as a final letter, *fala<u>r</u>* (fah-LAHŘ)
s,ss	**s** as in English '<u>s</u>ome': when initial, *<u>s</u>entir* (sehn-TEEHR); after a consonant, *pul<u>s</u>o* (POOHL-sooh); when written double, *cla<u>ss</u>e* (KLAH-sĭh); before unvoiced consonants (c [k], t), *e<u>s</u>cola* (ĭs-KAW-lah), *e<u>s</u>quecer* (ĭs-keh-SEHR), *e<u>s</u>tudar* (ĭs-tooh-DAHR);when absolutely final, *somo<u>s</u>* (SAW-moohs)
	z as in English '<u>z</u>eal,' when between two vowels: *coi<u>s</u>a* (KOY-zah), *o<u>s</u> amigos* (oohz-ah-MEEH-goos)
t	**t** as in English '<u>t</u>en'
u	**ooh** as in English 'r<u>u</u>le': *n<u>ú</u>mero* (NOOH-meh-rooh)
	w as in English '<u>w</u>ill' before or after another vowel: *líng<u>u</u>a* (LEEHN-gwah), *q<u>u</u>ando* (KWAHN-dooh)
v	**v** as in English '<u>v</u>ain': *<u>v</u>ida* (VEEH-dah)

Letter	Pronounced

x   **sh** as in English 'shall' when initial: *xadrez* (shah-DREHSS); sometimes between vowels, *baixo* (BAY-shooh)

    z as in English 'zeal' when in initial **ex** + vowel: *exemplo* (eh-ZEHM-plooh), *examinar* (eh-zah-meeh-NAHR)

    s as in English 'say' in initial **ex** + consonant: *excursão* (ehs-koohr-ZAH-OOHN); between two vowels in some words, like Portuguese **ss**, *trouxe* (TROH-seeh); and before a consonant, *sexto* (SEH-stooh)

z   **z** as in English 'zeal' when initial: *zêlo* (ZEH-looh); between two vowels, *fazer*, (*fah*-ZEHR); before a voiced consonant (b,d,g,m,n,r), *voz baixa* (voz-BAH-shah)

    s as in English 'say' before an unvoiced consonant (p, s, t): *voz passiva* (vohs-pah-SEEH-vah); when absolutely final *uma vez* (ooh-mah-VEHS)

Digraphs

ch	**sh** as in English 'shall': *chover* (shaw-VEHR)
lh	**ly** as in English 'filial': *ilha* (EEHL-yah)
nh	**ny** as in English 'onion': *vinho* (VEEHN-yooh)

Diphthongs

ai	**ay** as in English 'ice': *saiba* (SAY-bah)
éi	as two vowels, open **e+y**: *papéis* (pah-PEY-eehs)
ei	**ey** as in English 'they': *primeiro* (preeh-MEY-rooh)
ói	as two vowels, open **o+y**: *herói* (eh-ROH-ĭh)
oi	as two vowels, close **o+y**: *coisa* (KOY-zah)
au	**ow** as in English 'cow': *mau* (MOW as in 'cow')
éu	as two vowels, open **e+w**: *céu* (SEH-ooh)
eu	as two vowels, close **e+w**: *meu* (MEH-ooh)
ou	**o** as in English 'note': *soube* (SOH-beeh)
ui	as two vowels, **u** as in English 'rule' + y : *ruivo* (ROOH-ĭh-vooh)
iu,io	as two vowels, **i** as in English 'machine'+ y : *tio* (TEEH-yooh)
ão, -am	nasalized combination of eh + oohn: *estão* (eh-STAH-OOHN); -ahn in the verbal ending -am, *falam* (FAH-LAHN)
ãe	ah-ĭhns nasalized combination of **i** as in English 'ice' + y: *mães* (MAH-ĭhns)
õe	oy-ĭhn, nasalized combination of **o+y**: *põe* (POY-ĭhn)

Note: The capital letters indicate a stressed syllable. A raised superscript (-ĭhns,-eehs) indicates a diminished sound.

airplane **(o) avião**
(ooh) ah-veeh -AH *-oohn*

alligator **(o) jacaré**
(ooh) zhah-kah-REH

alphabet **(o) alphabeto**
(ooh) ahl-fah-BEH-tooh

antelope **(o) antilope**
(ooh) ahn-teeh-LO-pĭh

antlers **(as) pontas**
(as) POHN-tas

apple   **(a) maçã**
(ah) mah-SÄN

aquarium   **(o) aquario**
(ooh) ah-KWAH-reeh-ooh

arch   **(o) arco**
(ooh) AHR-kooh

arrow   **(a) flecha**
(ah) FLEH-shah

autumn   **(o) outono**
(ooh) oh-TOH-nooh

baby   **(a) criança**
(ah) kreeh-AHN-tsah

backpack   **(o) sacco de ombro**
(ooh) SAH-kooh-dĭh-OHM brooh

badger   **(o) texugo**
(ooh) teh-SHOOH-gooh

baker   **(o) padeiro**
(ooh) pah-DEY-rooh

ball   **(a) bola**
(ah) BOH-lah

balloon   **(o) balão**
(ooh) bah-LAH-ᵒᵒʰⁿ

banana   **(a) banana**
(ah) bah-NAH-nah

barley   **(a) cevada**
(ah) seh-VAH-dah

barrel   **(o) barril**
(ooh) bah-ŘEEHL

basket   **(a) cesta**
(ah) SEH-stah

bat   **(o) morcêgo**
(ooh) mohr-SEY-gooh

beach   **(a) praia**
(ah) PRAH-yah

bear　　　　　　　**(o) urso**
(ooh) OOHR-sooh

beaver　　　　　　**(o) castor**
(ooh) kah-STOHR

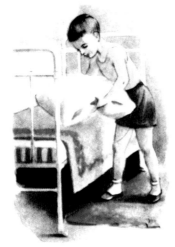

bed　　　　　　　**(a) cama**
(ah) KAH-mah

bee　　　　　　　**(a) abelha**
(ah) ah-BEHL-yah

beetle　　　　　　**(o) besouro**
(ooh) beh-ZOH-rooh

bell　　　　　　　**(a) campaihna**
(ah) kahm-pah-EEHN-yah

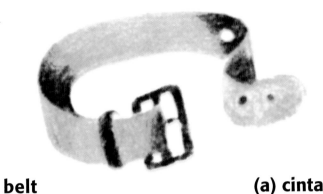

belt   **(a) cinta**
(ah) SEEHN-tah

bench   **(o) banco**
(ooh) BAHN-kooh

bicycle   **(a) bicicleta**
(ah) beeh-seeh-KLEH-tah

binoculars   **(o) binóculo**
(ooh) beeh-NAW-kooh-looh

bird   **(o) pássaro**
(ooh) PAH-sah-rooh

birdcage   **(a) gaiola**
(ah) gah-YAW-lah

black　　　　　　　　**prêto**
PREH-tooh

blocks　　　　　　　**(os) blocos**
(oohs) BLOH-koohs

blossom　　　　　　　**(a) flor**
(ah) FLAWR

blue　　　　　　　　**azul**
ah-ZOOHL

boat　　　　　　　　**(o) barco**
(ooh) BAHR-kooh

bone　　　　　　　　**(o) osso**
(ooh) AW-sooh

book   **(o) livro**
(ooh) LEEH-vrooh

boot   **(a) bota**
(ah) BAW-tah

bottle   **(a) garrafa**
(ah) gah-RAH-fah

bowl   **(a) tigela**
(ah) teeh-ZHEH-lah

boy   **(o) menino**
(ooh) ᵐⁱʰ-NEEH-nooh

bracelet   **(o) bracelete**
(ooh) brah-sĭh-LEH-tĭh

branch   **(o) ramo**
(ooh) RAH-mooh

bread   **(o) pão**
(ooh) PAH-ᵒᵒʰⁿ

breakfast   **(o) café-da-manhã**
*(ooh) kah-FEH-dah-mahn-YAH*ᴺ

bridge   **(o) ponte**
(ooh) POHN-tĭh

broom   **(a) vassoura**
(ah) vah-SOH-rah

brother   **(o) irmão**
(ooh) eehr-MAH-ᵒᵒʰⁿ

brown　　　　　　**castahno**
kah-STAHN-yooh

brush　　　　　　**(a) escôva**
(ah) ĭh-SKOH-vah

bucket　　　　　　**(o) balde**
(ooh) BAHL-dĭh

bulletin board　(o) quadro de avisos
(ooh) KWAH-drooh-deeh-ah-VEEH-zoohs

bumblebee　　　　　　**(o) abelhão**
(ooh) ah-behl-YAH-ᵒᵒʰⁿ

butterfly　　　　　　**(a) borboleta**
(ah) bawr-baw-LEH-tah

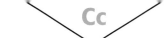

cab   **(o) táxi**
(ooh) TAHK-seeh

cabbage   **(o) couve**
(ooh) KOH-veeh

cactus   **(o) cacto**
(ooh) KAHK-tooh

café   **(o) bar**
(ooh) BAHR

cake   **(o) bólo**
(ooh) BOH-looh

camel   **(o) camelo**
(ooh) kah-MEH-looh

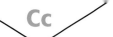

camera   **(a) câmara**
(ah) KAH-mah-rah

candle   **(a) vela**
(ah) VEH-lah

candy   **(o) doce**
(ooh) DOH-seeh

canoe   **(o) canoa**
(ooh) kah-NOH-ah

cap   **(o) boné**
(ooh) boh-NEH

captain   **(o) capitão**
(ooh) kah-peeh-TAH-oohn

car   **(o) automóvel**
(ooh) AH-ᵒᵒʰ-taw-MOH-vĭl

card   **(a) carta**
(ah) KAHR-tah

carpet   **(o) tapête**
(ooh) tah-PEH-tĭh

carrot   **(a) cenoura**
(ah) seh-NOH-rah

(to) carry   **levar**
leh-VAHR

castle   **(o) castelo**
(ooh) kah-STEH-looh

cat   **(o) gato**
(ooh) GAH-tooh

cave   **(a) gruta**
(ah) GROOH-tah

chair   **(a) cadeira**
(ah) kah-DEY-rah

cheese   **(o) queijo**
(ooh) KEY-zhooh

cherry   **(a) cereja**
(ah) seh-REY-zhah

chimney   **(o) chaminé**
(ooh) shah-meeh-NEH

chocolate **(o) chocolate**
(ooh) shoh-koh-LAH-teeh

Christmas tree **(a) árvore de Natal**
(ah) AHR-voh-rĭh-dĭ-nah-TAHL

circus **(o) circo**
(ooh) SEEHR-kooh

(to) climb **trepar**
trĭ-PAHR

cloud **(a) nuvem**
(ah) NOOH-vehn

clown **(o) palhaço**
(ooh) pahl-YAH-sooh

coach   **(o) côche**
(ooh) KOH-shee

coat   **(o) paletô**
(ooh) pah-ⁱⁱ-TOH

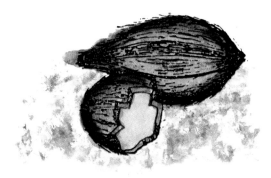

coconut   **(o) côco**
(ooh) KOH-kooh

comb   **(o) pente**
(ooh) PEHN-ᵗⁱ

comforter   **(o) acolchoado**
(ooh) ah-kohl-shoh-AH-dooh

compass   **(a) bússola**
(ah) BOOH-saw-lah

(to) cook   **cozinhar**
koh-zeehn-YAHR

cork   **(a) cortiça**
(ah) kohr-TEEH-sah

corn   **(o) milho**
(ooh) meehl-YOOH

cow   **(a) vaca**
(ah) VAH-kah

cracker   **(a) bolacha**
(ah) boh-LAH-shah

cradle   **(o) berço**
(ooh) BEHR-sooh

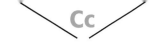

(to) crawl **engatinhar**
ehn-gah-teehn-YAHR

(to) cross **atravessar**
ah-trah-veh-SAHR

crown **(a) coroa**
(ah) koh-ROH-ah

(to) cry **chorar**
shaw-RAHR

cucumber **(o) pepino**
(ooh) peh-PEEH-nooh

curtain **(a) cortina**
(ah) kohr-TEEH-nah

(to) dance **bailar**
bay-LAHR

dandelion **(o) dente de leão**
(ooh) DEHN-tĭ-dĭ-leeh-AH-ᵒᵒʰⁿ

date **(a) data**
(ah) DAH-tah

deer **(o) cervo**
(ooh) SEHR-vooh

desert **(o) deserto**
(ooh) deh-ZEHR-tooh

desk **(a) escrivaninha**
(ah)-ĭ-screeh-vah-NEEHN-yah

dirty **sujo**
SOOH-zhooh

dog

(o) cachorro
(ooh) kah-SHAW-řooh

doghouse

(o) canil
(ooh) kah-NEEHL

doll

(a) boneca
(ah) booh-NEH-kah

dollhouse

(a) casa da boneca
(ah) KAH-zah-dah- booh-NEH-kah

dolphin

(o) delfim
(ooh) del-FEEH^N

donkey

(o) burro
(ooh) BOOH-rooh

dragon

(o) dragão
(ooh) drah-GOW-^{oohn}

dragonfly   **(a) libélula**
(ah) lĭ-BEH-looh-lah

(to) draw   **desenhar**
dĭ-zehn-YAHR

dress   **(o) vestido**
(ooh) veh-STEEH-dooh

(to) drink   **beber**
beh-BEHR

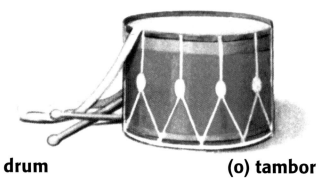

drum   **(o) tambor**
(ooh) tahm-BAWR

duck   **(o) pato**
(ooh) PAH-tooh

eagle

(a) águia
(ah) AH-gueeh-ah

(to) eat

comer
kaw-MEHR

egg

(o) ôvo
(ooh) OH-vooh

eggplant

(a) berinjela
(ah) beh-reehn-ZHEH-lah

eight

oito
OY-tooh

elbow

(o) cotovêlo
(ooh) koh-toh-VEH-looh

elephant

(o) elefante
(ooh) el-eh-FAHN-teeh

empty   **vazio**
vah-ZEEH-ooh

engine   **(a) máquina**
(ah) MAH-keeh-nah

envelope   **(o) envelope**
(ooh) ehn-veh-LAW-peeh

escalator   **(a) escada rolante**
(ah) ĭs-KAH-dah-řoh-LAHN-tĭh

Eskimo   **(o) esquimó**
(ooh) ehs-keeh-MAW

(to) explore   **explorar**
ehs-ploh-RAHR

eye   **(o) ôlho**
(ooh) OHL-yooh

face   **(a) cara**
(ah) KAH-rah

fan   **(o) ventilador**
(ooh) vehn-teeh-lah-DOHR

father   **(o) pai**
(ooh) PAH-ĭʰ

fear   **(o) mêdo**
(ooh) MEH-dooh

feather   **(a) pluma**
(ah) PLOOH-mah

(to) feed   **dar a comer**
dahr-ah-koh-MEHR

fence **(a) cêrca**
(ah) SEHR-kah

fern **(a) samambaia**
(ah) sah-mahm-BAH-yah

field **(o) campo**
(ooh) KAHM-pooh

field mouse **(o) arganaz**
(ooh) ahr-gah-NAHS

finger **(o) dedo**
(ooh) DEH-dooh

fir tree **(o) abeto**
(ooh) ah-BEH-tooh

fire **(o) fogo**
(ooh) FOH-gooh

fish **(o) peixe**
(ooh) PEY-sheeh

(to) fish **pescar**
pehs-KAHR

fist **(o) punho**
(ooh) POOHN-yooh

five **cinco**
SEEHN-kooh

flag **(a) bandeira**
(ah) bahn-DEY-rah

flashlight **(a) lanterna elétrica**
(ah) lahn-TEHR-nah-eh-LEH-trĭ-kah

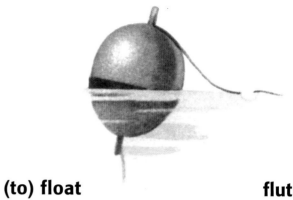

(to) float **flutuar**
flooh-tooh-AHR

flower **(a) flor**
(ah) FLAWR

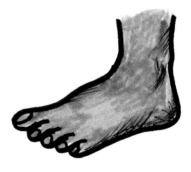

(to) fly **voar**
voh-AHR

foot **(o) pé**
(ooh) PEH

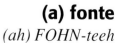

fork **(o) garfo**
(ooh) GAHR-fooh

fountain **(a) fonte**
(ah) FOHN-teeh

four   **quatro**
KWAH-trooh

fox   **(a) rapôsa**
(ah) rah-POH-zah

frame   **(a) moldura**
(ah) mohl-DOOH-rah

friend   **(o) amigo**
(ooh) ah-MEEH-gooh

frog   **(a) rã**
(ah) Rä^{n}

fruit   **(a) fruta**
(ah) FROOH-tah

furniture   **(a) mobília**
(ah) maw-BEEHL-^{i}-yah

garden **(o) jardim**
(ooh) zhahr-DEEH^n

gate **(o) portão**
(ooh) pohr-TAH-^{oohn}

(to) gather **colhêr**
kohl-YEH^r

geranium **(o) gerânio**
(ooh) zheh-RAHN^i-yooh

giraffe **(a) girafa**
(ah) zheeh-RAH-fah

girl **(a) môça**
(ah) MOH-sah

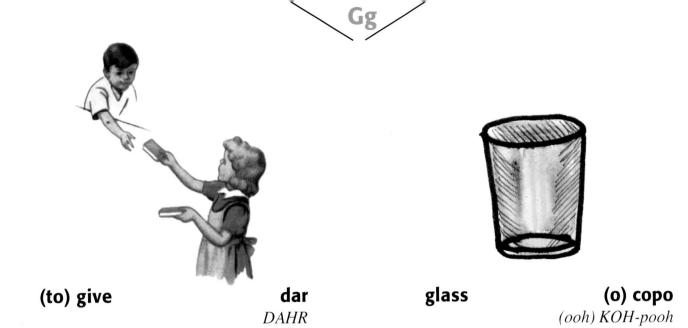

(to) give   **dar**
DAHR

glass   **(o) copo**
(ooh) KOH-pooh

glasses   **(os) óculos**
(oohs) AW-kooh-loohs

globe   **(o) globo**
(ooh) GLOH-booh

glove   **(a) luva**
(ah) LOOH-vah

goat   **(a) cabra**
(ah) KAH-brah

goldfish **(o) peixinho dourado**
(ooh) peh[i]-SHEEN-yooh-doh-RAH-dooh

"Good Night" **boa-noite**
BOH-ah-NOY-[ti]

"Good-bye" **adeus**
ah-DEH-oohs

goose **(o) ganso**
(ooh) GAHN-sooh

grandfather **(o) avô**
(ooh) ah-VOH

grandmother **(a) avó**
(ah) ah-VOH

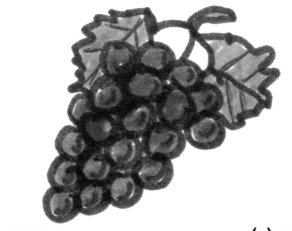

grapes　　　　　**(a) uva**
(ah) OOH-vah

grasshopper　　　**(o) gafanhoto**
(ooh) gah-fahn-YAW-tooh

green　　　　　**verde**
VEHR-dĭh

greenhouse　　　**(a) estufa**
(ah) ĭ-STOOH-fah

guitar　　　　　**(o) violão**
(ooh) veeh-oh-LAH-ᵒᵒʰⁿ

hammer   **(o) martelo**
(ooh) mahr-TEH-looh

hammock   **(a) rêde**
(ah) REH-dĭh

hamster   **(o) criceto**
(ooh) kreeh-SEH-tooh

hand   **(a) mão**
(ah) MAH-oohn

handbag   **(a) bolsa**
(ah) BOHL-sah

handkerchief   **(o) lenço**
(ooh) LEHN-sooh

harvest **(a) colheita**
(ah) kohl-YEY-tah

hat **(o) chapéu**
(ooh) shah-PEH -ooh

hay **(o) feno**
(ooh) FEH-nooh

headdress **(a) touca**
(ah) TOH-kah

heart **(o) coração**
(ooh) koh-rah-SAH-oohn

hedgehog **(o) porco-espinho**
(ooh) PAWR-kĭh-SPEEHN-yooh

hen   **(a) galinha**
(ah) gah-LEEHN-yah

(to) hide   **esconder-se**
es-kon-DEHR-sĭ

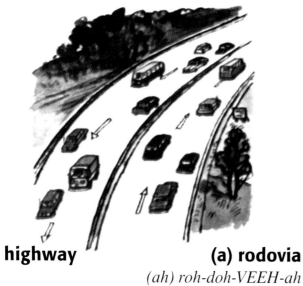

highway   **(a) rodovia**
(ah) roh-doh-VEEH-ah

honey   **(o) mel**
(ooh) MEH[L]

horns   **(os) côrnos**
(oohs) KOHR-noohs

horse   **(o) cavalo**
(ooh) kah-VAH-looh

horseshoe **(a) ferradura**
(ah) feh-rah-DOOH-rah

hourglass **(a) ampulheta**
(ah) ahm-poohl-YEH-tah

house **(a) casa**
(ah) KAH-zah

(to) hug **abraçar**
ah-brah-SAHR

hydrant **(o) hidrante**
(ooh) eeh-DRAHN-teeh

ice cream **(o) sorvete**
(ooh) sohr-VEH-tĭ

ice cubes **(os) cubos de gêlo**
(oos) KOOH-boohs-dĭ-ZHEH-looh

ice-skating **patinação sôbre o gêlo**
pah-teeh-nah-SAH-ᵒᵒʰⁿ- SAW-brĭh-ooh-ZHEH-looh

instrument **(o) instrumento**
(ooh) eehn-strooh-MEHN-tooh

iris **(a) íris**
(ah) EEH-reehs

iron **(o) ferro a passar roupa**
(ooh) FEH-rooh-ah-pah-SAHR-ROH-pah

island **(a) ilha**
(ah) EEHL-yah

jacket   **(a) jaqueta**
(ah) zhah-KEH-tah

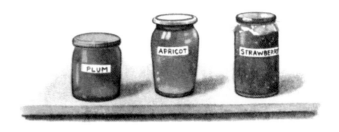

jam   **(a) geléia de frutas**
(ah) zheh-LEH-ah-dĭ-FROOH-tahs

jigsaw puzzle   **(o) quebra-cabeça**
(ooh) KEH-brah-kah-BEH-sah

jockey   **(o) joquei**
(ooh) ZHOH-key

juggler   **(o) malabarista**
(ooh) mah-lah-bah-REEH-stah

(to) jump   **saltar**
sahl-TAHR

kangaroo   **(o) cangurú**
(ooh) kahn-gooh-ROOH

key   **(a) chave**
(ah) SHAH-veeh

kitten   **(o) gatinho**
(ooh) gah-TEEHN-yooh

knife   **(a) faca**
(ah) FAH-kah

knight   **(o) paladino**
(ooh) pah-lah-DEEHN-ooh

(to) knit   **tricotar**
treeh-koh-TAHR

knot   **(o) nó**
(ooh) NAW

koala bear   **(o) koala**
(ooh) koh-AH-lah

ladder   **(a) escada**
(ah) ĭh-SKAH-dah

ladybug   **(a) joaninha**
(ah) zhoh-ah-NEEHN-yah

lamb   **(o) cordeiro**
(ooh) kohr-DEY-rooh

lamp   **(a) lâmpada**
(ah) LAHM-pah-dah

(to) lap   **marulhar**
mah-roohl-YAHR

laughter   **(a) risada**
(ah) řeeh-ZAH-dah

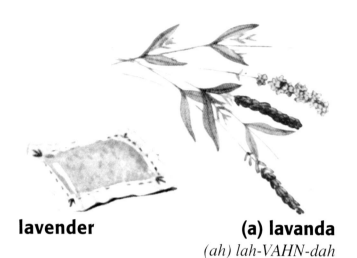

lavender   **(a) lavanda**
(ah) lah-VAHN-dah

lawn mower   **(o) cortador de grama**
(ooh) kohr-tah-DOHR-dĭ-GRAH-mah

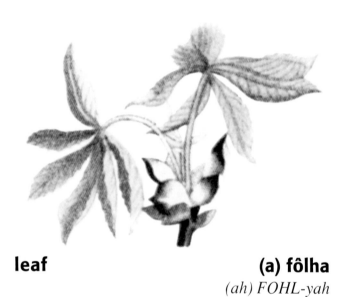

leaf   **(a) fôlha**
(ah) FOHL-yah

leg   **(a) perna**
(ah) PEHR-nah

lemon   **(o) limão**
(ooh) leeh-MAH-ᵒᵒʰⁿ

lettuce   **(a) alface**
(ah) ahl-FAH-sĭh

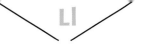

lightbulb **(a) lâmpada elétrica**
(ah) LAHM-pah-dah-eh-LEH-trĭh-kah

lighthouse **(o) farol**
(ooh) fah-ROHL

lilac **(o) lilás**
(ooh) lee-LAHS

lion **(o) leão**
(ooh) lĭ-AH-oohn

(to) listen **escutar**
ĭ-skooh-TAHR

lobster **(a) lagosta**
(ah) lah-GOH-stah

lock   **(a) fechadura**
(ah) feh-shah-DOOH-rah

lovebird   **(o) periquito**
(ooh) peh-reeh-KEEH-tooh

luggage   **(a) bagagem**
(ah) bah-GAH-zheh^n

lumberjack   **(o) lenhador**
(ooh) lehn-yah-DOHR

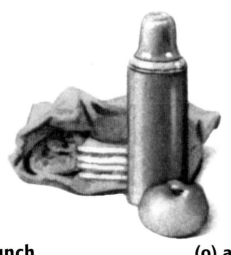

lunch   **(o) almôço**
(ooh) ahl-MOH-^{sooh}

lynx   **(o) lince**
(ooh) LEEHN-sĭh

magazine   **(a) revista**
(ah) reh-VEEH-stah

magician   **(o) mago**
(ooh) MAH-gooh

magnet   **(o) magneto**
(ooh) mahg-NEH-tooh

map   **(o) mapa**
(ooh) MAH-pah

maple leaf   **(a) fôlha de bôrdo**
(ah) FOHL-yah-dĭ-BOHR-dooh

marketplace   **(o) mercado**
(ooh) mehr-KAH-dooh

mask   **(a) máscara**
(ah) MAH-skah-rah

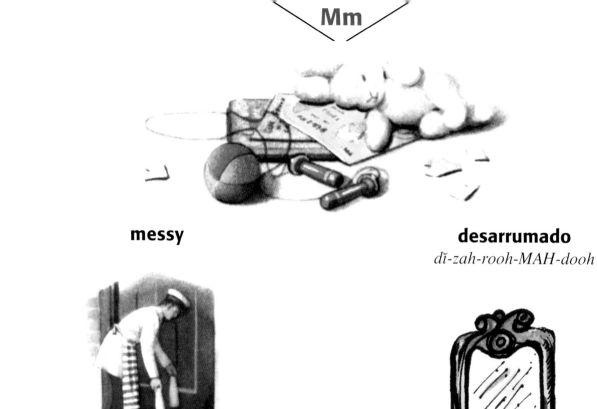

messy

desarrumado
dǐ-zah-rooh-MAH-dooh

milkman

(o) leiteiro
(ooh) ley-TEY-rooh

mirror

(o) espelho
(ooh) ǐh-SPEHL-yooh

mitten

(a) miteni
(ah) mǐ-TEH-neeh

money

(o) dinheiro
(ooh) deehn-YEY-rooh

monkey

(o) macaco
(ooh) mah-KAH-kooh

moon

(a) lua
(ah) LOOH-ah

mother **(a) mãe**
(ah) MAH-ĭhn

mountain **(a) montanha**
(ah) mohn-TAHN-yah

mouse **(o) camundongo**
(ooh) kah-moohn-DOHN-gooh

mouth **(a) bôca**
(ah) BOH-kah

mushroom **(o) cogumelo**
(ooh) koh-gooh-MEH-looh

music **(a) música**
(ah) MOOH-zeeh-kah

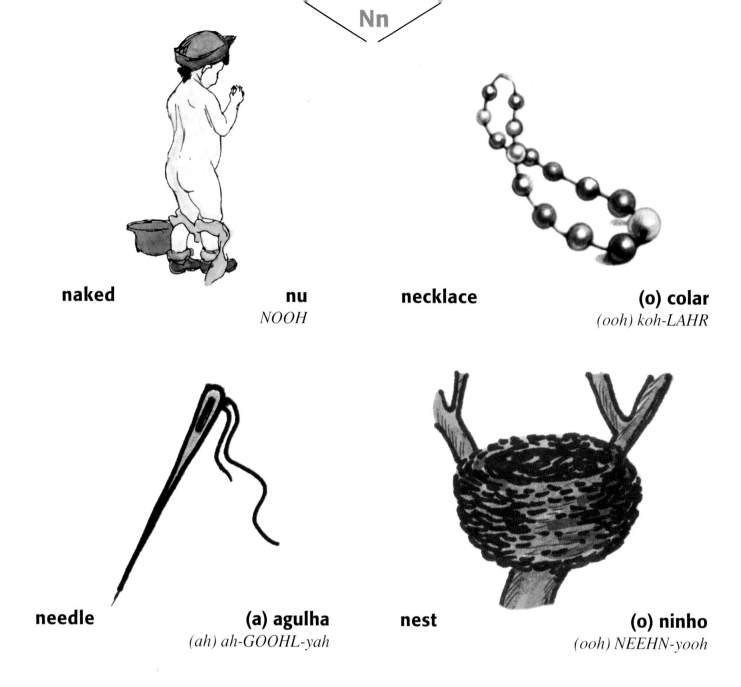

naked   **nu**
NOOH

necklace   **(o) colar**
(ooh) koh-LAHR

needle   **(a) agulha**
(ah) ah-GOOHL-yah

nest   **(o) ninho**
(ooh) NEEHN-yooh

newspaper   **(o) jornal**
(ooh) zhoor-NAHL

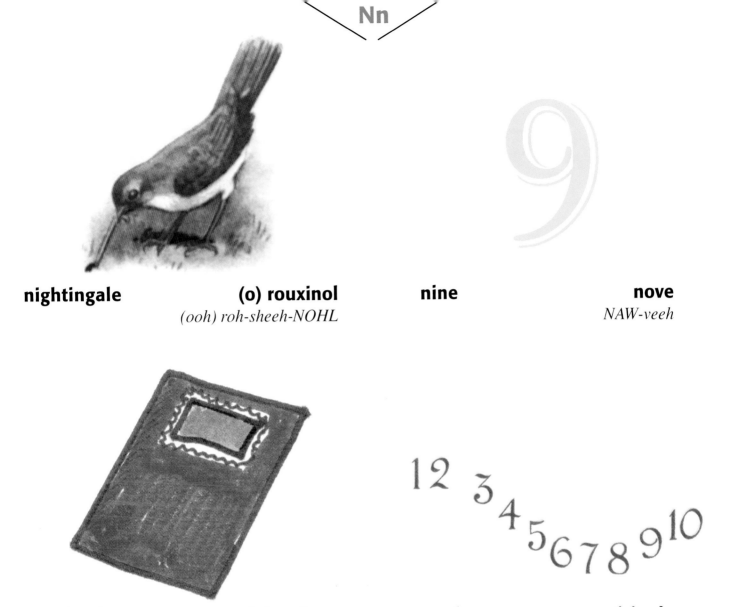

nightingale **(o) rouxinol**
(ooh) roh-sheeh-NOHL

nine **nove**
NAW-veeh

notebook **(o) caderno**
(ooh) kah-DEHR-nooh

number **(o) número**
(ooh) NOOH-meh-rooh

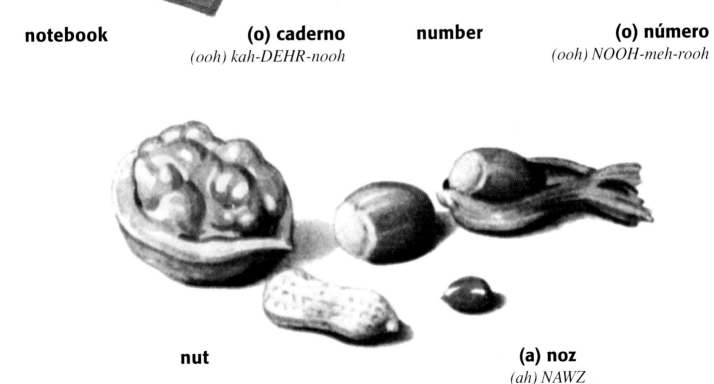

nut **(a) noz**
(ah) NAWZ

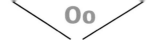

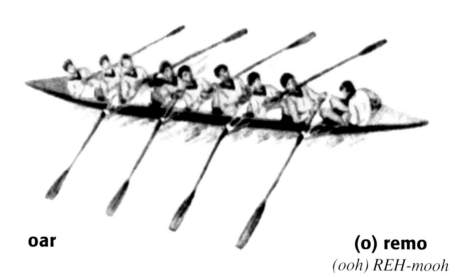

oar　　　　　　**(o) remo**
(ooh) REH-mooh

ocean liner　　　**(o) transatlântico**
(ooh) trahns-aht-LAHN-teeh-kooh

old　　　　　　　**velho**
VEHL-yooh

one　　　　　**uno**
OOH-nooh

onion　　　　**(a) cebola**
(ah) seh-BOH-lah

open   **aberto**
ah-BEHR-tooh

orange   **(a) laranja**
(ah) lah-RÄN-zhah

ostrich   **(o) avestruz**
(ooh) ah-veh-STROOHS

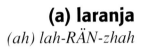

owl   **(a) coruja**
(ah) koh-ROOH-zhah

ox   **(o) boi**
(ooh) BOY

padlock   **(o) cadeado**
(ooh) kah-dĭ-AH-dooh

paint   **(a) tinta**
(ah) TEEHN-tah

painter

(o) pintor
(ooh) peehn-TOHR

pajamas   **(o) pijama**
(ooh) peeh-ZHAH-mah

palm tree   **(a) palmeira**
(ah) pahl-MEY-rah

paper   **(o) papel**
(ooh) pah-PEHL

parachute   **(o) pára-quedas**
(ooh) pah-rah-KEH-dahs

park   **(o) parque**
(ooh) PAHR-keeh

parrot   **(o) papagaio**
(ooh) pah-pah-GAH-yooh

passport   **(o) passaporte**
(ooh) pah-sah-POHR-tĭh

patch   **(o) remendo**
(ooh) reh-MEHN-dooh

path   **(a) senda**
(ah) SEHN-dah

peach   **(o) pêssego**
(ooh) PEH-seh-gooh

pear   **(a) pêra**
(ah) PEH-rah

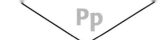

pebble **(o) seixo**
(ooh) SEY-shooh

(to) peck **bicar**
beeh-KAHR

(to) peel **descascar**
dehs-kahs-KAHR

pelican **(o) pelicano**
(ooh) peh-leeh-KAH-nooh

penguin **(o) pingüim**
(ooh) peehn-GWEEH^N

pencil **(o) lápis**
(ooh) LAH-pĭs

people **(a) gente**
(ah) ZHEN-tĭh

piano   **(o) piano**
(ooh) peeh-AH-nooh

pickle   **(o) picles**
(ooh) PEEH-clĭhs

pie   **(a) torta**
(ah) TAWR-tah

pig   **(o) porco**
(ooh) POHR-kooh

pigeon   **(o) pombo**
(ooh) POH^M-booh

pillow   **(o) travesseiro**
(ooh) trah-veh-SEY-rooh

pin   **(o) alfinête**
(ooh) ahl-feeh-NEH-tĭh

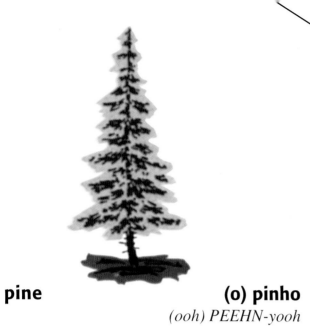

pine   **(o) pinho**
(ooh) PEEHN-yooh

pineapple   **(o) abacaxí**
(ooh) ah-bah-kah-SHEEH

pit   **(o) caroço**
(ooh) kah-ROH-sooh

pitcher   **(o) jarro**
(ooh) ZHAH-řooh

plate   **(o) prato**
(ooh) PRAH-tooh

platypus   **(o) ornitorrinco**
(ooh) OHR-neeh-toh-REEHN-kooh

(to) play   **jogar**
zhoh-GAHR

plum   **(a) ameixa**
(ah) ah-MEY-shah

polar bear   **(o) urso branco**
(ooh) OOHR-sooh-BRAHN-kooh

pony   **(o) pônei**
(ooh) POH-ney

pot   **(a) panela**
(ah) pah-NEH-lah

potato   **(a) batata**
(ah) bah-TAH-tah

(to) pour **vazar**
vah-ZAHR

present **(o) presente**
(ooh) preh-ZEHN-tĭh

(to) pull **puxar**
pooh-SHAHR

pumpkin **(a) abóbora-moganga**
(ah) ah-BOH-boh-rah-moh-GAHN-gah

Qq

puppy **(o) cachorinho**
(ooh) kah-shoh-REEHN-yooh

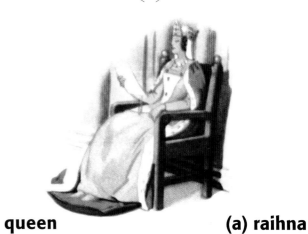

queen **(a) raihna**
(ah) rah-EEHN-yah

rabbit

(o) coelho
(ooh) KWEHL-yooh

raccoon

(o) procionídeo
(ooh) proh-seeh-oh-NEEH-deh-oh

racket

(a) raqueta
(ah) rah-KEH-tah

radio

(o) rádio
(ooh) RAH-ᵈⁱYOH

radish

(o) rabanete
(ooh) rah-bah-NEH-tǐh

raft   **(a) jangada**
(ah) zhan-GAH-dah

rain   **(a) chuva**
(ah) SHOOH-vah

rainbow   **(o) arco-íris**
(ooh) AHR-koh-EEH-reehs

raincoat   **(o) impermeável**
(ooh) eehm-pehr-meh-AH-vehl

raspberry   **(a) framboesa**
(ah) frahm-BWEH-ZAH

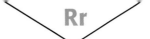

(to) read   **ler**
LEHR

red   **vermelho**
vehr-MEHL-yooh

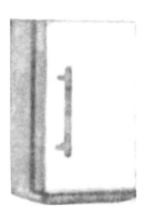

refrigerator   **(a) geladeira**
(ah) zheh-lah-DEY-rah

rhinoceros   **(o) rinoceronte**
(ooh) reeh-noh-seh-ROHN-tǐ

ring   **(o) anel**
(ooh) ah-NEHL

(to) ring　　　**sonar**
soh-NAHR

river　　　**(o) rio**
(ooh) REEH-ooh

road　　　**(a) estrada**
(ah) ĭ-STRAH-dah

rocket　　　**(o) foguete**
(ooh) foh-GHEH-teeh

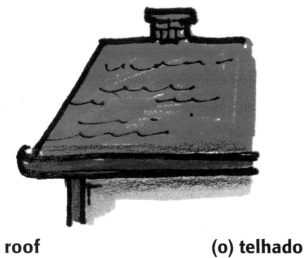

roof　　　**(o) telhado**
(ooh) tehl-YAH-dooh

rooster　　　**(o) galo**
(ooh) GAH-looh

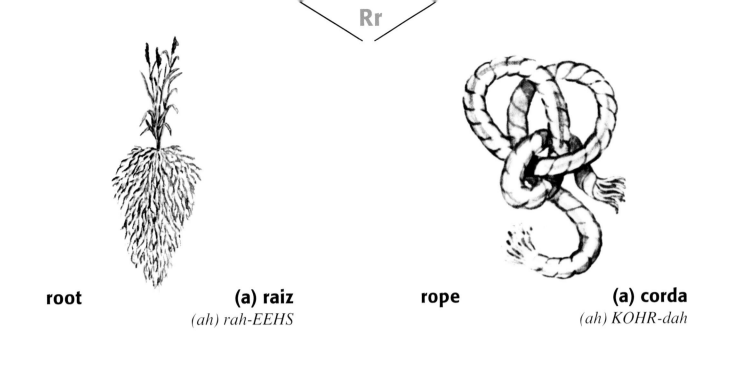

root   **(a) raiz**
(ah) rah-EEHS

rope   **(a) corda**
(ah) KOHR-dah

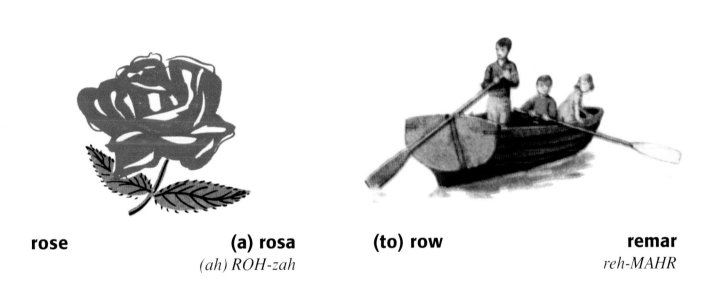

rose   **(a) rosa**
(ah) ROH-zah

(to) row   **remar**
reh-MAHR

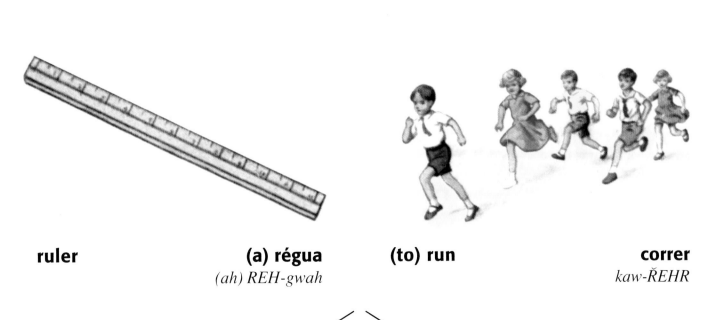

ruler   **(a) régua**
(ah) REH-gwah

(to) run   **correr**
kaw-ŘEHR

safety pin   (o) alfinête de segurança
(ooh) ahl-feeh-NEH-teeh-dĭ-sĭ-gooh-RAHN-sah

(to) sail   **navegar**
nah-vĭ-GAHR

sailor   **(o) marinheiro**
(ooh) mah-reehn-YEY-rooh

salt   **(o) sal**
(ooh) SAH^L

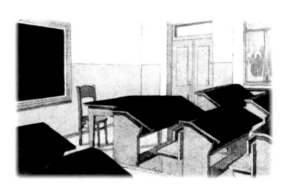

scarf   **(a) charpa**
(ah) SHAHR-pah

school   **(a) escola**
(ah) ĭs-KOH-lah

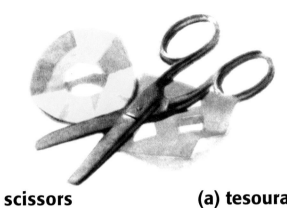

scissors   **(a) tesoura**
(ah) tĭh-ZOH-rah

screwdriver   **(a) chave de fenda**
(ah) SHAH-veeh-dĭ-FEHN-dah

seagull   **(a) gaivota**
(ah) gay-VOH-tah

seesaw   **(a) gangorra**
(ah)gahn-GOH-řah

seven   **sete**
SEH-tĭ

(to) sew   **coser**
kaw-ZEHR

shark   **(o) tubarão**
(ooh) tooh-bah-RAH^OOHN

sheep   **(o) carneiro**
(ooh) kahr-NEY-rooh

shell   **(a) concha**
(ah) KOHN-shah

shepherd   **(o) pastor**
(ooh) pah-STOHR

ship   **(o) navio**
(ooh) nah-VEEH-ooh

shirt   **(a) camisa**
(ah) kah-MEEH-zah

shoe   **(o) sapato**
(ooh) sah-PAH-tooh

shovel   **(a) pá**
(ah) PAH

(to) show   **mostrar**
moh-STRAHR

shower   **(o) chuveiro**
(ooh) shooh-VEY-rooh

shutter   **(a) veneziana**
(ah) veh-neh-zeeh-AH-nah

sick   **doente**
doh-EHN-tĭh

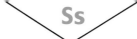

sieve   **(a) peneira**
(ah) peh-NEY-rah

(to) sing   **cantar**
kahn-TAHR

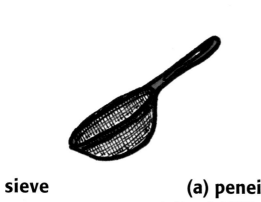

(to) sit   **sentar**
sehn-TAHR

six   **seis**
SEY^S

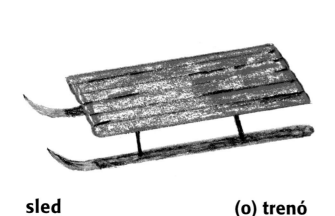

sled   **(o) trenó**
(ooh) treh-NOH

(to) sleep   **dormir**
dohr-MEEHR

small   **pequeno**

pĭh-KEH-nooh

smile   **(o) sorriso**

(ooh) soh-REEH-zooh

snail   **(o) caracol**

(ooh) kah-rah-KOHL

snake   **(o) serpente**

(ooh) sehr-PEHN-tĭh

snow   **(a) neve**

(ah) NEH-veeh

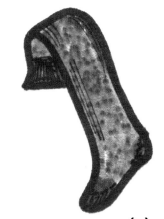

sock   **(o) soquete**

(ooh) saw-KEH-tĭh

sofa   **(o) sofá**
(ooh) soh-FAH

sparrow   **(o) pardal**
(ooh) pahr-DAHL

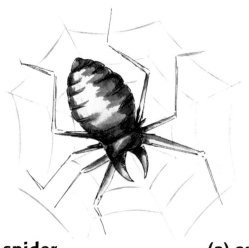

spider   **(a) aranha**
(ah) ah-RAHN-yah

spiderweb   **(a) teia de aranha**
(ah) TEY-ah-deeh-ah-RAHN-yah

spoon   **(a) colher**
(ah) kohl -YEHR

squirrel   **(o) esquilo**
(ooh) es-KEEH-looh

stairs   **(a) escada**
(ah) ĭh-SKAH-dah

stamp   **(o) sêlo**
(ooh) SEH-looh

starfish   **(a) estrêla do mar**
(ah) ĭh-STREH-lah-dooh-MAHR

stork   **(a) cegonha**
(ah) sĭh-GOH^N -yah

stove   **(o) fogão a gás**
(ooh) foh-GAH^{oohn}-ah-GAHS

strawberry   **(o) morango**
(ooh) moh-RAHN-gooh

subway

(o) metró
(ooh) meh-TROH

sugar cube   **(o) cubo de açucar**
(ooh) KOOH-booh-dĭ-ah-SOOH-kahr

sun

(o) sol
(ooh) SOHL

sunflower   **(o) girassol**
(ooh) zheeh-rah-SOHL

sweater

(a) suéter
(ah) SWEH-tehr

(to) sweep   **varrer**
vah-ŘEHR

swing

(o) balanço
(ooh) bah-LAHN-sooh

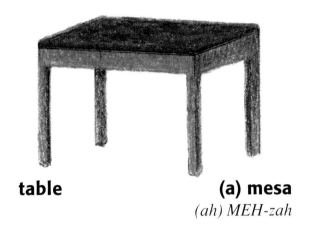

table   **(a) mesa**
(ah) MEH-zah

teapot   **(o) bule de chá**
*(ooh) BOOH-*ˡĭˉ *dĭh-SHAH*

teddy bear   **(o) ursinho**
(ooh) oohr-SEEHN-yooh

television   **(a) televisão**
*(ah) teh-leh-veeh-ZAH*ᴼᴼᴴᴺ

10

ten   **dez**
DEHZ

tent   **(a) tenda**
(ah) TEHN-dah

theater   **(o) teatro**
(ooh) tĭ-AH-trooh

thimble   **(o) dedal**
(ooh) deh-DAHL

(to) think   **pensar**
pehn-SAHR

three   **três**
TREHS

tie   **(a) gravata**
(ah) grah-VAH-tah

(to) tie   **atar**
ah-TAHR

tiger   **(o) tigre**
(ooh) TEEH-grĭh

toaster   **(a) torradeira**
(ah) toh-řah-DEY-rah

tomato   **(o) tomate**
(ooh) toh-MAH-tĭh

toucan   **(o) tucano**
(ooh) tooh-KAH-nooh

towel   **(a) toalha**
(ah) tooh-AHL-yah

tower   **(a) tôrre**
(ah) TOH-řĭh

toy box   (a) caixa de brinquedos
(ah) KAY-shah-dĭh-breehn-KEH-doohs

tracks   (os) trilhos
(oohs) TREEHL-yoohs

train station   (a) estação
(ah) ĭh-stah-SAH^{oohn}

tray   (a) bandeja
(ah) bahn-DEH-zhah

tree   (a) árvore
(ah) AHR-voh-rĭh

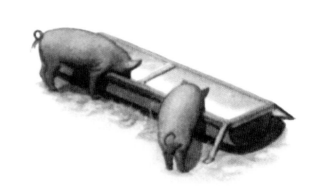

trough   (a) gamela
(ah) gah-MEH-lah

truck   **(o) caminhão**
(ooh) kah-meehn-YAH^(oohn)

trumpet   **(a) trombeta**
(ah) trohm-BEH-tah

tulip   **(a) tulipa**
(ah) tooh-LEEH-pah

tunnel   **(o) túnel**
(ooh) TOOH-nehl

turtle   **(a) tartaruga**
(ah) tahr-tah-ROOH-gah

twins   **(os) gêmeos**
(oohs) ZHE-meh-oohs

two   **dois**
DOYS

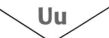

umbrella   **(o) guarda-chuva**
(ooh) gwahr-dah-SHOOH-vah

uphill   **(a) ascensão**
(ah) ah-sehn-SAH^{oohn}

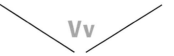

Vv

vase   **(o) vaso**
(ooh) VAH-zooh

veil   **(o) véu**
(ooh) VEH-ooh

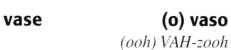

village   **(a) aldeia**
(ah) ahl-DEY-ah

violet   **(a) violeta**
(ah) veeh-oh-LEH-tah

violin   **(o) violino**
(ooh) veeh-ooh-LEEH-nooh

voyage   **(a) viagem**
(ah) veeh-AH-zhehn

waiter   **(o) garção**
(ooh) gahr-SAH^oohn

(to) wake up   **despertar**
deh-spehr-TAHR

walrus   **(a) morsa**
(ah) MOHR-sah

(to) wash   **lavar**
lah-VAHR

watch   **(o) relógio**
(ooh) reh-LOH-zhooh

(to) watch   **guardar**
gwahr-DAHR

(to) water   **regar**
reh-GAHR

waterfall   **(a) cachoeira**
(ah) kah-shooh - EY-rah

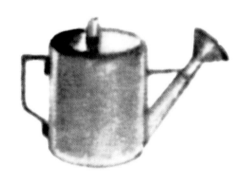

watering can   **(o) regador**
(ooh) reh-gah-DOHR

watermelon   **(a) melancia**
(ah) meh-lahn-SEEH-ah

weather vane   **(o) cata-vento**
(ooh) kah-tah-VEHN-tooh

(to) weigh   **pesar**
peh-ZAHR

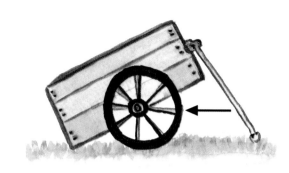

whale   **(a) baleia**
(ah) bah-LEH-ah

wheel   **(a) roda**
(ah) ROH-dah

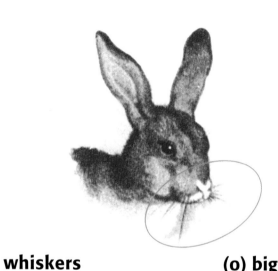

wheelbarrow   **(o) carrinho de mão**
(ooh) kah-ŘEEHN-yooh-dĭ-MAH^{OOHN}

whiskers   **(o) bigode**
(ooh) beeh-GOH-dĭh

(to) whisper   **cochichar**
koh-sheeh-SHAHR

whistle   **(o) assovio**
(ooh) ah-SOH-^{vĭ}ooh

white   **branco**
BRAHN-kooh

wig   **(a) peruca**
(ah) peh-ROOH-kah

wind   **(o) vento**
(ooh) VEHN-tooh

window   **(a) janela**
(ah) zhah-NEH-lah

wings   **(as) alas**
(ahs) AH-lahs

winter   **(o) inverno**
(ooh) eehn-VEHR-nooh

wolf **(o) lôbo**
(ooh) LOH-booh

wood **(a) madeira**   **word** **(a) palavra**
(ah) mah-DEY-rah   *(ah) pah-LAH-vrah*

(to) write **escrever**
ĭs-kreh-VEHR

yellow   **amarelo**
ah-mah-REH-looh

Zz

zebra   **(a) zêbra**
(ah) ZEH-brah

A

abacaxí (o) pineapple
abelha (a) bee
abelhão (o) bumblebee
aberto open
abeto (o) fir tree
abóbora-moganga (a) pumpkin
abraçar (to) hug
acolchoado (o) comforter
adeus "Good-bye"
águia (a) eagle
agulha (a) needle
alas (as) wings
aldeia (a) village
alface (a) lettuce
alfinête (o) pin
alfinête de segurança (o) safety pin
almôço (o) lunch
alphabeto (o) alphabet
amarelo yellow
ameixa (a) plum
amigo (o) friend
ampulheta (a) hourglass
anel (o) ring
antilope (o) antelope
aquario (o) aquarium
aranha (a) spider
arco (o) arch
arco-íris (o) rainbow
arganaz (o) field mouse
árvore (a) tree
árvore de Natal (a) Christmas tree
ascensão (a) uphill
assovio (o) whistle
atar (to) tie
atravessar (to) cross
automóvel (o) car
avestruz (o) ostrich
avião (o) airplane
avô (o) grandfather
avó (a) grandmother
azul blue

B

bagagem (a) luggage
bailar (to) dance
balanço (o) swing
balão (o) balloon
balde (o) bucket
baleia (a) whale
banana (a) banana
banco (o) bench
bandeira (a) flag
bandeja (a) tray
bar (o) café
barco (o) boat
barril (o) barrel
batata (a) potato
beber (to) drink
berço (o) cradle
berinjela (a) eggplant
besouro (o) beetle
bicar (to) peck
bicicleta (a) bicycle
bigode (o) whiskers
binóculo (o) binoculars
blocos (os) blocks
boa-noite "Good night"
bôca (a) mouth
boi (o) ox
bola (a) ball
bolacha (a) cracker
bólo (o) cake
bolsa (a) handbag
boné (o) cap
boneca (a) doll
borboleta (a) butterfly
bota (a) boot
bracelete (o) bracelet
branco white
bule de chá (o) teapot
burro (o) donkey
bússola (a) compass

C

cabra (a) goat
cachoeira (a) waterfall

cachorinho (o) puppy
cachorro (o) dog
cacto (o) cactus
cadeado (o) padlock
cadeira (a) chair
caderno (o) notebook
café-da-manhã (o) breakfast
caixa de brinquedos (a) toy box
cama (a) bed
câmara (a) camera
camelo (o) camel
caminhão (o) truck
camisa (a) shirt
campaihna (a) bell
campo (o) field
camundongo (o) mouse
cangurú (o) kangaroo
canil (o) doghouse
canoa (o) canoe
cantar (to) sing
capitão (o) captain
cara (a) face
caracol (o) snail
carneiro (o) sheep
caroço (o) pit
carrinho de mão (o) wheelbarrow
carta (a) card
casa (a) house
casa da boneca (a) dollhouse
castahno brown
castelo (o) castle
castor (o) beaver
cata-vento (o) weather vane
cavalo (o) horse
cebola (a) onion
cegonha (a) stork
cenoura (a) carrot
cêrca (a) fence
cereja (a) cherry
cervo (o) deer
cesta (a) basket
cevada (a) barley

chaminé (o) chimney
chapéu (o) hat
charpa (a) scarf
chave (a) key
chave de fenda (a) screwdriver
chocolate (o) chocolate
chorar (to) cry
chuva (a) rain
chuveiro (o) shower
cinco five
cinta (a) belt
circo (o) circus
côche (o) coach
cochichar (to) whisper
côco (o) coconut
coelho (o) rabbit
cogumelo (o) mushroom
colar (o) necklace
colheita (a) harvest
colher (a) spoon
colhêr (to) gather
comer (to) eat
concha (a) shell
copo (o) glass
coração (o) heart
corda (a) rope
cordeiro (o) lamb
côrnos (os) horns
coroa (a) crown
correr (to) run
cortador de grama (o) lawn mower
cortiça (a) cork
cortina (a) curtain
coruja (a) owl
coser (to) sew
cotovêlo (o) elbow
couve (o) cabbage
cozinhar (to) cook
criança (a) baby
criceto (o) hamster
cubo de açucar (o) sugar cube
cubos de gêlo (os) ice cubes

D

dar (to) give
dar a comer (to) feed
data (a) date
dedal (o) thimble
dedo (o) finger
delfim (o) dolphin
dente de leão (o) dandelion
desarrumado messy
descascar (to) peel
desenhar (to) draw
deserto (o) desert
despertar (to) wake up
dez ten
dinheiro (o) money
doce (o) candy
doente sick
dois two
dormir (to) sleep
dragão (o) dragon

E

elefante (o) elephant
engatinhar (to) crawl
envelope (o) envelope
escada (a) ladder, stairs
escada rolante (a) escalator
escola (a) school
esconder-se (to) hide
escôva (a) brush
escrever (to) write
escrivaninha (a) desk
escutar (to) listen
espelho (o) mirror
esquilo (o) squirrel
esquimó (o) Eskimo
estação (a) train station
estrada (a) road
estrêla do mar (a) starfish
estufa (a) greenhouse
explorar (to) explore

F

faca (a) knife
farol (o) lighthouse
fechadura (a) lock
feno (o) hay
ferradura (a) horseshoe
ferro a passar roupa (o) iron
flecha (a) arrow
flor (a) blossom, flower
flutuar (to) float
fogão a gás (o) stove
fogo (o) fire
foguete (o) rocket
fôlha (a) leaf
fôlha de bôrdo (a) maple leaf
fonte (a) fountain
framboesa (a) raspberry
fruta (a) fruit

G

gafanhoto (o) grasshopper
gaiola (a) birdcage
gaivota (a) seagull
galinha (a) hen
galo (o) rooster
gamela (a) trough
gangorra (a) seesaw
ganso (o) goose
garção (o) waiter
garfo (o) fork
garrafa (a) bottle
gatinho (o) kitten
gato (o) cat
geladeira (a) refrigerator
geléia de frutas (a) jam
gêmeos (os) twins
gente (a) people
gerânio (o) geranium
girafa (a) giraffe

girassol (o) sunflower
globo (o) globe
gravata (a) tie
gruta (a) cave
guardar (to) watch
guarda-chuva (o) umbrella

H

hidrante (o) hydrant

I

ilha (a) island
impermeável (o) raincoat
instrumento (o) instrument
inverno (o) winter
íris (a) iris
irmão (o) brother

J

jacaré (o) alligator
janela (a) window
jangada (a) raft
jaqueta (a) jacket
jardim (o) garden
jarro (o) pitcher
joaninha (a) ladybug
jogar (to) play
joquei (o) jockey
jornal (o) newspaper

K

koala (o) koala bear

L

lagosta (a) lobster
lâmpada (a) lamp
lâmpada elétrica (a) lightbulb
lanterna elétrica (a) flashlight
lápis (o) pencil

laranja (a) orange
lavanda (a) lavender
lavar (to) wash
leão (o) lion
leiteiro (o) milkman
lenço (o) handkerchief
lenhador (o) lumberjack
ler (to) read
levar (to) carry
libélula (a) dragonfly
lilás (o) lilac
limão (o) lemon
lince (o) lynx
livro (o) book
lôbo (o) wolf
lua (a) moon
luva (a) glove

M

maçã (a) apple
macaco (o) monkey
madeira (a) wood
mãe (a) mother
magneto (o) magnet
mago (o) magician
malabarista (o) juggler
mão (a) hand
mapa (o) map
máquina (a) engine
marinheiro (o) sailor
martelo (o) hammer
marulhar (to) lap
máscara (a) mask
mêdo (o) fear
mel (o) honey
melancia (a) watermelon
menino (o) boy
mercado (o) marketplace
mesa (a) table
metró (o) subway
milho (o) corn
miteni (a) mitten
mobília (a) furniture

môça (a) girl
moldura (a) frame
montanha (a) mountain
morango (o) strawberry
morcêgo (o) bat
morsa (a) walrus
mostrar (to) show
música (a) music

N

navegar (to) sail
navio (o) ship
neve (a) snow
ninho (o) nest
nó (o) knot
nove nine
noz (a) nut
nu naked
número (o) number
nuvem (a) cloud

O

óculos (os) glasses
oito eight
ôlho (o) eye
ornitorrinco (o) platypus
osso (o) bone
outono (o) autumn
ôvo (o) egg

P

pá (a) shovel
padeiro (o) baker
pai (o) father
paladino (o) knight
palavra (a) word
paletô (o) coat
palhaço (o) clown
palmeira (a) palm tree
panela (a) pot
pão (o) bread
papagaio (o) parrot
papel (o) paper
pára-quedas (o) parachute
pardal (o) sparrow
parque (o) park
passaporte (o) passport
pássaro (o) bird
pastor (o) shepherd
patinação sôbre o gêlo ice-skating
pato (o) duck
pé (o) foot
peixe (o) fish
peixinho dourado (o) goldfish
pelicano (o) pelican
peneira (a) sieve
pensar (to) think
pente (o) comb
pepino (o) cucumber
pequeno small
pêra (a) pear
periquito (o) lovebird
perna (a) leg
peruca (a) wig
pesar (to) weigh
pescar (to) fish
pêssego (o) peach
piano (o) piano
picles (o) pickle
pijama (o) pajamas
pingüim (o) penguin
pinho (o) pine
pintor (o) painter
pluma (a) feather
pombo (o) pigeon

pônei (o) pony
pontas (as) antlers
ponte (o) bridge
porco (o) pig
porco-espinho (o) hedgehog
portão (o) gate
praia (a) beach
prato (o) plate
presente (o) present
prêto black
procionídeo (o) raccoon
punho (o) fist
puxar (to) pull

Q

quadro de avisos (o) bulletin board
quatro four
quebra-cabeça (o) jigsaw puzzle
queijo (o) cheese

R

rã (a) frog
rabanete (o) radish
rádio (o) radio
raihna (a) queen
raiz (a) root
ramo (o) branch

rapôsa (a) fox
raqueta (a) racket
rêde (a) hammock
regador (o) watering can
regar (to) water
régua (a) ruler
relógio (o) watch
remar (to) row
remendo (o) patch
remo (o) oar
revista (a) magazine
rinoceronte (o) rhinoceros
rio (o) river
risada (a) laughter
roda (a) wheel
rodovia (a) highway
rosa (a) rose
rouxinol (o) nightingale

S

sacco de ombro (o) backpack
sal (o) salt
saltar (to) jump
samambaia (a) fern
sapato (o) shoe
seis six
seixo (o) pebble
sêlo (o) stamp
senda (a) path
sentar (to) sit
serpente (o) snake
sete seven
soar (to) ring
sofá (o) sofa
sol (o) sun
soquete (o) sock
sorriso (o) smile
sorvete (o) ice cream
suéter (a) sweater
sujo dirty

T

tambor (o) drum
tapête (o) carpet
tartaruga (a) turtle
táxi (o) cab
teatro (o) theater
teia de aranha (a) spiderweb
televisão (a) television
telhado (o) roof
tenda (a) tent
tesoura (a) scissors
texugo (o) badger
tigela (a) bowl
tigre (o) tiger
tinta (a) paint
toalha (a) towel
tomate (o) tomato
torradeira (a) toaster
tôrre (a) tower
torta (a) pie
touca (a) headdress
transatlântico (o) ocean liner
travesseiro (o) pillow
trenó (o) sled
trepar (to) climb
três three
tricotar (to) knit
trilhos (os) tracks
trombeta (a) trumpet
tubarão (o) shark
tucano (o) toucan
tulipa (a) tulip
túnel (o) tunnel

U

uno one
ursinho (o) teddy bear
urso (o) bear
urso branco (o) polar bear
uva (a) grapes

V

vaca (a) cow
varrer (to) sweep
vaso (o) vase
vassoura (a) broom
vazar (to) pour
vazio empty
vela (a) candle
velho old
veneziana (a) shutter
ventilador (o) fan
vento (o) wind
verde green
vermelho red
vestido (o) dress
véu (o) veil
viagem (a) voyage
violão (o) guitar
violeta (a) violet
violino (o) violin
voar (to) fly

Z

zêbra (a) zebra

Folk Tales from Bohemia
Adolf Wenig
This folk tale collection is one of a kind, focusing uniquely on humankind's struggle with evil in the world. Delicately ornate red and black text and illustrations set the mood.
Ages 9 and up
90 pages • red and black illustrations • 5 1/2 x 8 1/4 • 0-7818-0718-2 • W • $14.95hc • (786)

Czech, Moravian and Slovak Fairy Tales
Parker Fillmore
Fifteen different classic, regional folk tales and 23 charming illustrations whisk the reader to places of romance, deception, royalty, and magic.
Ages 12 and up
243 pages • 23 b/w illustrations • 5 1/2 x 8 1/4 • 0-7818-0714-X • W • $14.95 hc • (792)

Glass Mountain: Twenty-Eight Ancient Polish Folk Tales and Fables
W.S. Kuniczak
Illustrated by Pat Bargielski
As a child in a far-away misty corner of Volhynia, W.S. Kuniczak was carried away to an extraordinary world of magic and illusion by the folk tales of his Polish nurse.
171 pages • 6 x 9 • 8 illustrations • 0-7818-0552-X • W • $16.95hc • (645)

Old Polish Legends
Retold by F.C. Anstruther
Wood engravings by J. Sekalski
This fine collection of eleven fairy tales, with an introduction by Zymunt Nowakowski, was first published in Scotland during World War II.
66 pages • 7 1/4 x 9 • 11 woodcut engravings • 0-7818-0521-X • W • $11.95hc • (653)

Folk Tales from Russia
by Donald A. Mackenzie
With nearly 200 pages and 8 full-page black-and-white illustrations, the reader will be charmed by these legendary folk tales that symbolically weave magical fantasy with the historic events of Russia's past.
Ages 12 and up
192 pages • 8 b/w illustrations • 5 1/2 x 8 1/4 • 0-7818-0696-8 • W • $12.50hc • (788)

Fairy Gold: A Book of Classic English Fairy Tales
Chosen by Ernest Rhys
Illustrated by Herbert Cole
Forty-nine imaginative black and white illustrations accompany thirty classic tales, including such beloved stories as "Jack and the Bean Stalk" and "The Three Bears."
Ages 12 and up
236 pages • 5 1/2 x 8 1/4 • 49 b/w illustrations • 0-7818-0700-X • W • $14.95hc • (790)

Tales of Languedoc: From the South of France

Samuel Jacques Brun

For readers of all ages, here is a masterful collection of folk tales from the south of France.

Ages 12 and up

248 pages • 33 b/w sketches • 5 1/2 x 8 1/4 • 0-7818-0715-8 • W • $14.95hc • (793)

Twenty Scottish Tales and Legends

Edited by Cyril Swinson

Illustrated by Allan Stewart

Twenty enchanting stories take the reader to an extraordinary world of magic harps, angry giants, mysterious spells and gallant Knights.

Ages 9 and up

215 pages • 5 1/2 x 8 1/4 • 8 b/w illustrations • 0-7818-0701-8 • W • $14.95 hc • (789)

Swedish Fairy Tales

Translated by H. L. Braekstad

A unique blending of enchantment, adventure, comedy, and romance make this collection of Swedish fairy tales a must-have for any library.

Ages 9 and up

190 pages • 21 b/w illustrations • 51/2 x 81/4 • 0-7818-0717-4 • W • $12.50hc • (787)

The Little Mermaid and Other Tales

Hans Christian Andersen

Here is a near replica of the first American edition of 27 classic fairy tales from the masterful Hans Christian Andersen.

Ages 9 and up

508 pages • b/w illustrations • 6 x 9 • 0-7818-0720-4 • W • $19.95hc • (791)

Pakistani Folk Tales: Toontoony Pie and Other Stories

Ashraf Siddiqui and Marilyn Lerch

Illustrated by Jan Fairservis

In these 22 folk tales are found not only the familiar figures of folklore—kings and beautiful princesses—but the magic of the Far East, cunning jackals, and wise holy men.

Ages 7 and up

158 pages • 6 1/2 x 8 1/2 • 38 illustrations • 0-7818-0703-4 • W • $12.50hc • (784)

Folk Tales from Chile

Brenda Hughes

This selection of 15 tales gives a taste of the variety of Chile's rich folklore. Fifteen charming illustrations accompany the text.

Ages 7 and up

121 pages • 5 1/2 x 8 1/4 • 15 illustrations • 0-7818-0712-3 • W • $12.50hc • (785)

All prices subject to change. **To purchase Hippocrene Books** contact your local bookstore, call (718) 454-2366, or write to: HIPPOCRENE BOOKS, 171 Madison Avenue, New York, NY 10016. Please enclose check or money order, adding $5.00 shipping (UPS) for the first book and $.50 for each additional book.